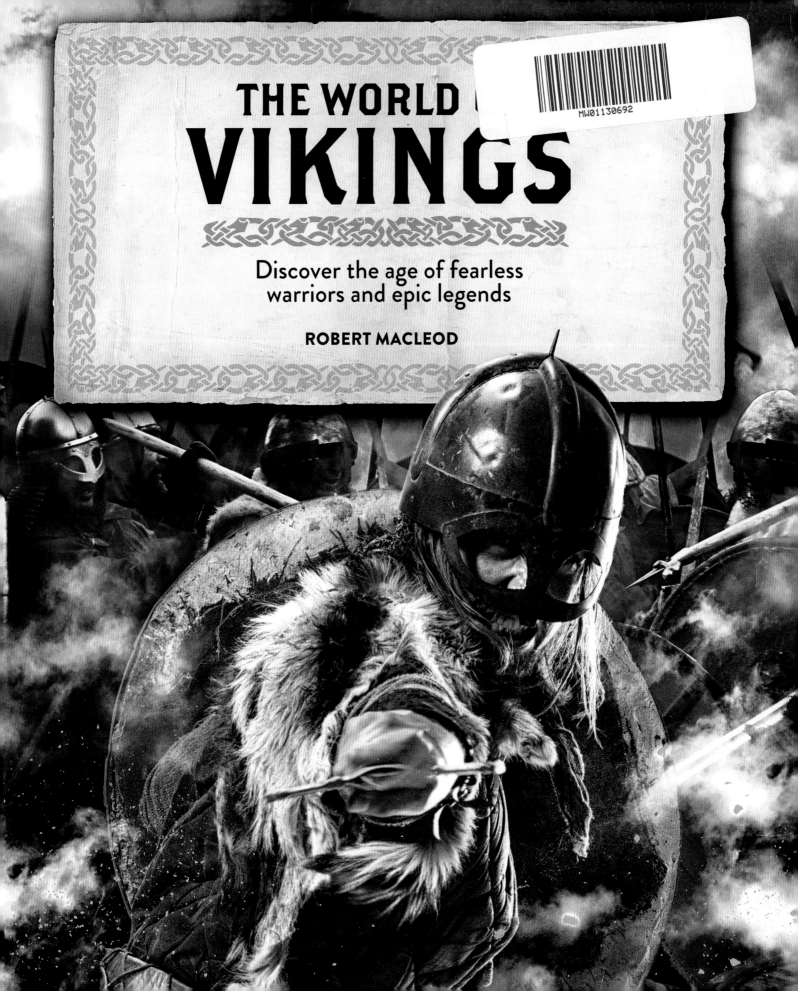

THE WORLD OF VIKINGS

Discover the age of fearless warriors and epic legends

ROBERT MACLEOD

CONTENTS

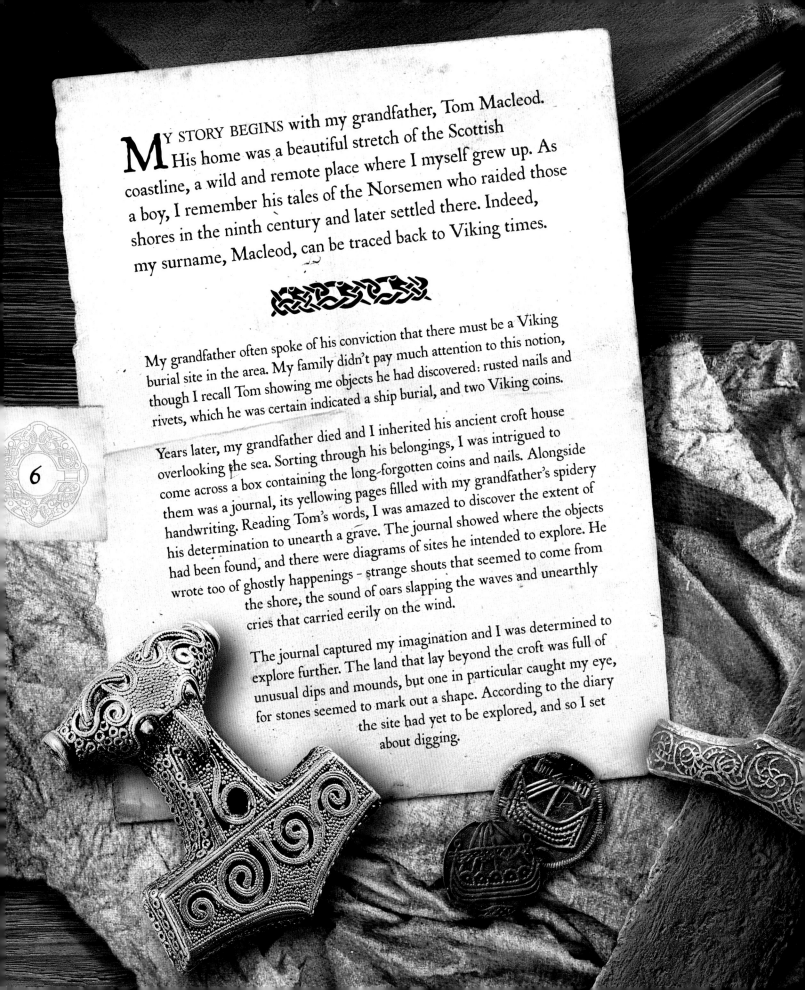

MY STORY BEGINS with my grandfather, Tom Macleod. His home was a beautiful stretch of the Scottish coastline, a wild and remote place where I myself grew up. As a boy, I remember his tales of the Norsemen who raided those shores in the ninth century and later settled there. Indeed, my surname, Macleod, can be traced back to Viking times.

My grandfather often spoke of his conviction that there must be a Viking burial site in the area. My family didn't pay much attention to this notion, though I recall Tom showing me objects he had discovered: rusted nails and rivets, which he was certain indicated a ship burial, and two Viking coins.

Years later, my grandfather died and I inherited his ancient croft house overlooking the sea. Sorting through his belongings, I was intrigued to come across a box containing the long-forgotten coins and nails. Alongside them was a journal, its yellowing pages filled with my grandfather's spidery handwriting. Reading Tom's words, I was amazed to discover the extent of his determination to unearth a grave. The journal showed where the objects had been found, and there were diagrams of sites he intended to explore. He wrote too of ghostly happenings - strange shouts that seemed to come from the shore, the sound of oars slapping the waves and unearthly cries that carried eerily on the wind.

The journal captured my imagination and I was determined to explore further. The land that lay beyond the croft was full of unusual dips and mounds, but one in particular caught my eye, for stones seemed to mark out a shape. According to the diary the site had yet to be explored, and so I set about digging.

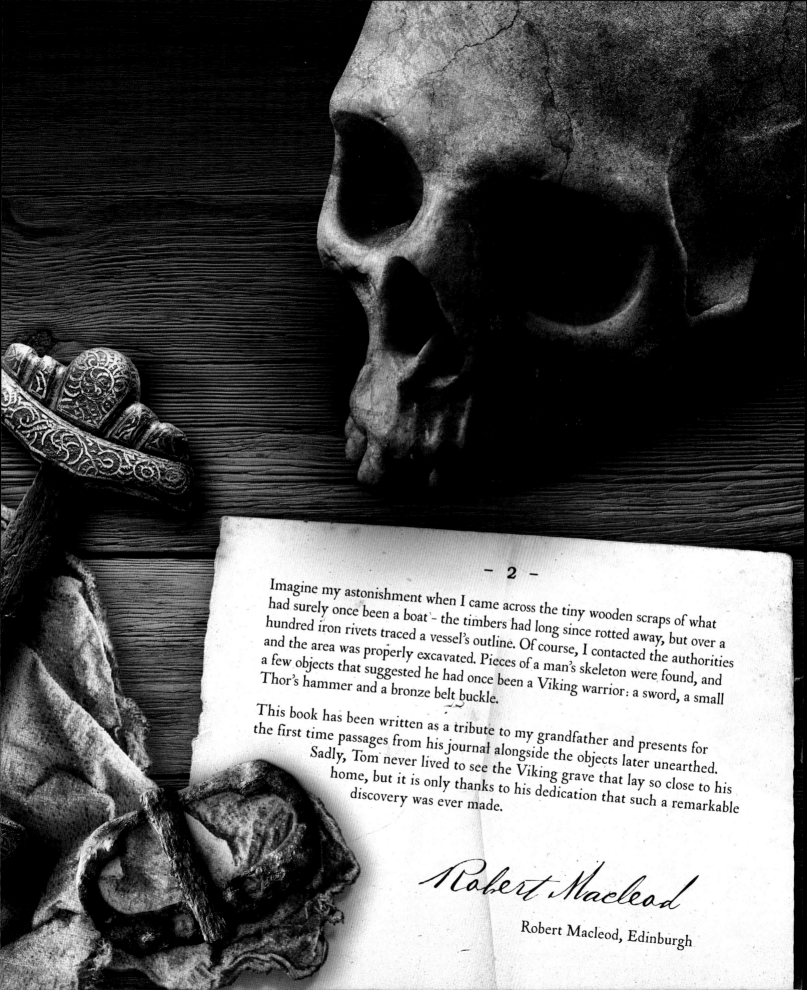

- 2 -

Imagine my astonishment when I came across the tiny wooden scraps of what had surely once been a boat - the timbers had long since rotted away, but over a hundred iron rivets traced a vessel's outline. Of course, I contacted the authorities and the area was properly excavated. Pieces of a man's skeleton were found, and a few objects that suggested he had once been a Viking warrior: a sword, a small Thor's hammer and a bronze belt buckle.

This book has been written as a tribute to my grandfather and presents for the first time passages from his journal alongside the objects later unearthed. Sadly, Tom never lived to see the Viking grave that lay so close to his home, but it is only thanks to his dedication that such a remarkable discovery was ever made.

Robert Macleod

Robert Macleod, Edinburgh

THE AGE OF VIKINGS

This lonely stretch of coastline has been my home for nearly 80 years now. Though the wind moans eerily around the cliffs and the sea is often wild, there is quiet here. Indeed, I can only imagine the shock and dread that rippled from village to village when Vikings first raided these shores. Across this land and far beyond, such terror arrived from the seas again and again. It is small wonder then that the people of those times had a prayer: "From the fury of the Northmen, deliver us O Lord..."

Tom Macleod

(An extract from the diary of Tom Macleod)

THE VIKING WORLD

MORE THAN 1,200 YEARS AGO, the Vikings set history ablaze. For 300 years, warriors from Norway, Denmark and Sweden spread terror across Europe as they raided for precious treasures and seized new land. The Vikings valued glory in battle above all, but they were far more than ruthless fighters. Merchants traded goods in places as far away as Baghdad (in modern-day Iraq), while daring explorers crossed dangerous waters in search of new lands, even reaching North America. The Vikings were also superb craftsmen - skilled woodworkers built swift ships, while expert metalworkers crafted sharp swords and axes as well as creating beautiful jewellery.

TIMELINE

789 AD – 899 AD

789:
The first recorded Viking attacks occur along the coasts of northern Europe and southern Britain.

793:
Vikings carry out a brutal attack on the monastery of Lindisfarne, an island off the north-east coast of England.

845:
Danish Vikings sack Paris in France and Hamburg in Germany.

c. 860:
The Viking chieftain Rurik the Rus becomes ruler of Novgorod in Russia.

900 AD – 999 AD

911:
The French give Normandy to the Viking leader Rollo.

954:
Eric Bloodaxe, the last Viking king of York, is killed at the Battle of Stainmore in England.

1000 AD – 1066 AD

1000:
Iceland becomes Christian.

1002:
Leif Erikson explores the coast of North America.

1014:
Olaf Haraldsson seizes the Norwegian throne.

795:
The Vikings begin to attack Scotland and Ireland.

800:
Vikings settle the Scottish islands of Orkney and Shetland, and discover the Faroe Islands.

840:
The Viking city of Dublin is founded in Ireland.

844:
The Vikings attack Spain but are driven away.

c. 872:
Harald Finehair becomes the first king of Norway.

865–74:
The Great Army from Denmark invades and conquers much of England.

874:
Vikings settle Iceland.

886:
King Alfred agrees a boundary between his kingdom and land in the north and east of England ruled by the Vikings (known as the "Danelaw").

c. 958:
Harald Bluetooth becomes king of Denmark. He converts to Christianity, and the religion begins to spread across Scandinavia.

c. 982–85:
Erik the Red discovers and settles Greenland.

1042:
Danish rule in England ends.

1016–30:
The Danish chieftain Cnut becomes king of England, and later king of Denmark and Norway.

1046:
Harald Hardrada becomes king of Norway.

1066:
Harald Hardrada, the "last great Viking", invades England but is killed in battle. The Normans conquer England. The Viking age draws to a close.

THE VIKING WORLD

As raiders, traders and explorers, the Vikings ventured far beyond their Scandinavian homelands. They attacked monasteries and towns across Europe, and crossed vast areas of unknown waters to explore and settle lands in the west. In the East, the Vikings made long and dangerous journeys along the rivers of central Europe into Russia, finally reaching the great cities of Constantinople (the heart of the Byzantine empire) and Baghdad.

Wherever they settled, the Vikings left behind not only archaeological remains and artefacts but a rich legacy that can be seen today in place names, folk tales and local customs.

14

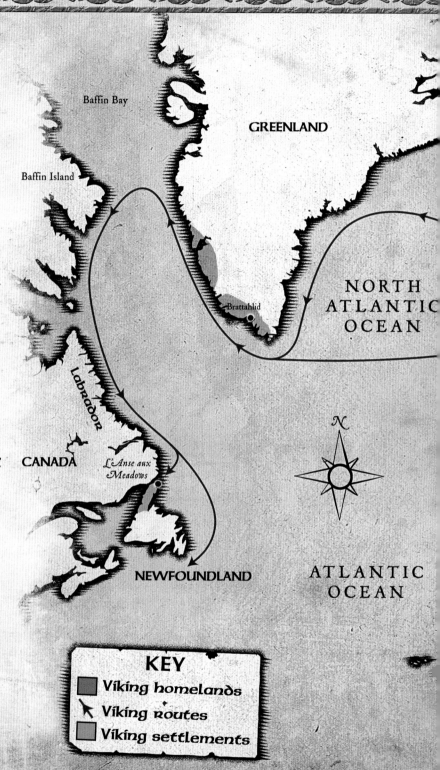

Baffin Bay

GREENLAND

Baffin Island

Brattahlid

NORTH ATLANTIC OCEAN

Labrador

CANADA

L'Anse aux Meadows

NEWFOUNDLAND

ATLANTIC OCEAN

N

KEY
- Viking homelands
- Viking routes
- Viking settlements

ARCTIC
OCEAN

...LAND

...avik

Faroe Islands

North Sea

NORWAY

SWEDEN

Kaupang

Birka

Novgorod

RUSSIA

SCOTLAND

Lindisfarne

DENMARK

Dublin

York

IRELAND

Hedeby

Hamburg

ENGLAND

GERMANY

Kiev

Paris

Normandy

FRANCE

Caspian Sea

ITALY

Black Sea

SPAIN

Byzantine Empire

Constantinople

Baghdad

Mediterranean Sea

NORTH AFRICA

VIKING HISTORY

ALTHOUGH THE VIKINGS did not leave behind any written documents, letters carved on stone or wood called "runes" provide clues about their traditions. More detail can be found in the writings of people who came into contact with the Vikings, but since they were often the victims of raids, their accounts can be unreliable. The Vikings told tales of their adventures that were passed on and eventually written down by Christian scholars in books called "sagas". These writings tell us much about the Vikings' spirit of adventure.

This Swedish rune stone was erected by a Viking in memory of his father. There are over 6,000 known rune stones across Scandinavia.

Ruins of the Brattahlid settlement on Greenland. Vikings lived on this island for over 400 years.

What's in a Name?

Experts disagree about where the word "Viking" comes from. Today the word is used for all Scandinavians of the Viking period, but the Old Norse word *vikingr* was used only for those who went raiding and plundering, or *i viking*. In Old Norse, *vik* meant "bay", and perhaps the word Viking came about because raiders sometimes lay in wait for their victims in sheltered bays and inlets.

The Anglo-Saxon Chronicle

The Anglo-Saxon Chronicle is a collection of manuscripts written by monks between the early ninth century and 1154, and provides a year-by-year account of what happened in the British Isles during this time. The writings contain vivid descriptions of Viking raids. For example, in 793 AD, the Chronicle records: "... the ravaging of heathen men destroyed God's church at Lindisfarne through brutal robbery and slaughter..."

A page from the Anglo-Saxon Chronicle describes how King Aethelred I of Wessex battled with invading Vikings during the ninth century.

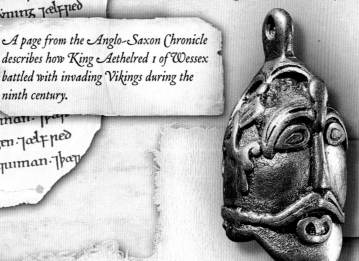

A Swedish pendant dating from the early Viking period.

Clues in the Landscape

The best evidence about the Vikings' way of life comes from archaeology. Discoveries at sites such as Jorvik (modern-day York in England) show what Viking houses were like, while animal bones and seeds provide clues to what people ate. The Vikings buried their dead with valued personal belongings, and items found in graves such as jewellery and weapons tell us much about daily life. Beautifully preserved ships have been discovered in burial mounds, and experts are able to work out where the Vikings travelled and traded by studying objects - such as coins - that they left behind.

Objects such as these coins, shears, comb and arm ring provide clues about the Vikings' way of life.

17

Exploring the World

19

The Vikings unleashed terrible violence upon these shores, but it is well to remember that they were far more than warriors. I have heard much of their incredible voyages to distant lands, and am fascinated by their daring and endurance. Imagine sailing across the open ocean without so much as a map or a compass! Raging storms and icy waters no doubt claimed the lives of many, but for some, the excitement of sighting new land would have been just reward for their courage.

Tom Macleod

(An extract from the diary of Tom Macleod)

VIKING SHIPS

THE VIKINGS built several different kinds of ship. Most famous of all are the long and slender "dragonboats" that swiftly carried warriors across the seas to launch surprise attacks. Sturdier cargo vessels called "knarrs" were used for long ocean voyages while slimmer cargo ships were built for carrying goods along the coast. For everyday life, the Vikings relied on small rowing boats.

These Viking boat rivets were discovered in Canada.

The beautiful Gokstad ship was excavated in Norway in 1880.

Viking warships under full sail.

Warships varied in length from 17.5 m to 36 m. The knarr, used for long voyages, had plenty of space for cargo while smaller cargo boats carried goods up and down the coast. Rowing boats were miniature versions of large ships, and were often carried on board larger vessels.

Large warship

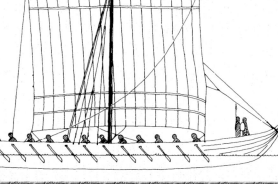

Skilled Shipbuilders

The secret of the Viking ship lay in its unique construction and all vessels followed the same basic design. Expert woodworkers split tree trunks - usually oak - into long thin planks. These were then shaped and fastened to a single keel (the supporting base of the ship) by iron nails, and then joined to each other, one board overlapping the next to create the body of the ship. This design is called the "clinker" technique, and meant that the boats were strong enough to carry a tall mast and big sail, yet light enough to be rowed very fast.

Masters of the Sea

Nobody really knows how the Vikings managed to cross thousands of miles of stormy waters without the aid of charts or compasses. They sailed within sight of land wherever possible, but when out in the open ocean they would have relied upon the sun, moon and stars to calculate their position. Viking navigators must have had an excellent understanding of wind and wave patterns, and would have learnt to recognize sea birds and fish to help them find their way to distant lands.

A weather vane (for showing wind direction) from a Viking ship mast.

Long-distance knarr boat

Coastal cargo boat

Small rowing boat (faering)

Discovering New Lands

THE VIKINGS were fearless explorers, leaving the safety of their shores to travel thousands of miles in search of new lands. These adventurers were mainly from Norway where there was a shortage of good farmland. As they braved the icy waters of the North Atlantic, many crews and ships were lost in terrible storms, but this didn't stop the Vikings reaching Iceland, Greenland and eventually North America.

Baffin Bay

Baffin Island

GREENLAND

Brattahlid

CANADA

NORTH ATLANT

L'Anse aux Meadows

Newfoundland

A reconstruction of a Viking longhouse in Iceland. The original was buried under volcanic ash.

A statue of Ingolf Arnarson in Reykjavik.

The Vikings in Iceland

The first settler to arrive on the volcanic island of Iceland was a Norwegian called Ingolf Arnarson. He took his family there around 874 AD and built a large farm on a bay. This later became Iceland's capital, Reykjavik. By 930 AD, more than 10,000 Vikings had arriv on the island. They lived mai along the green and fertile coast – the harsh interior, wit its mountains, volcanoes and glaciers, remained uninhabite

ARCTIC OCEAN

ICELAND

Rkjavik

Faroe Islands

NORWAY

SWEDEN

BRITISH ISLES

DENMARK

The Vikings first discovered the Faroe Islands and Iceland, then made their way further west to Greenland and North America.

The Brattahlid settlement in Greenland. Erik the Red's home stood somewhere here.

Erik the Red

Land of Ice and Snow

The most famous Viking to explore Greenland was Erik the Red. This rocky island is covered in snow and ice, but Erik discovered an ice-free region on the south-west coast with good grazing. To attract settlers he named it Greenland. In 985 AD, he persuaded Icelandic Vikings to move to the island with him and more soon followed. Despite the harsh climate, the settlers were able to grow barley, and keep sheep and cattle. Walrus tusks, arctic fox furs and polar bear skins were exported and exchanged for metals, tools and timber. The Vikings thrived in Greenland for over 400 years - experts are not sure why they eventually deserted the island, but perhaps isolation and the increasingly cold climate drove them away.

Arctic fox fur

LEIF ERIKSON

PERHAPS one of the most famous explorers of all time, Leif Erikson is remembered in the sagas as a daring hero. Travelling across the stormy Atlantic Ocean, he became the first European to reach North America around 1002 AD. Fellow Vikings believed that Leif was surely favoured by the gods, and his spirit of adventure and good fortune in the face of danger earned him the nickname "Leif the Lucky".

Born to Explore

Leif was born into a family of explorers around 980 AD. His father was the great adventurer Erik the Red who first settled Greenland around 985 AD. Around this time, Erik heard the intriguing tale of an Icelander named Bjarni Herjolfsson who set sail for Greenland but was blown far off course. Sailing west, Bjarni was amazed to glimpse a new coastline and returned to Greenland with the exciting news.

The Land of Wine

Leif grew up hearing about the famed land that lay west of Greenland. As soon as he was able, the young explorer gathered a crew together to retrace Bjarni's route. Along the way, Leif found and named three lands. Helluland (Flatstone Land) was probably Baffin Island and Markland (Land of Woods) was almost certainly Labrador in Canada. Eventually the men found a suitable place to set up camp and named this lush new land Vinland (Wineland) after the wild grapes growing there. After several months, Leif and his crew returned safely to Greenland, but other Vikings later journeyed to Vinland, some staying for years at a time.

The Mysterious Land

For centuries, scholars believed that the stories of Vinland were nothing more than fables. However, in 1961, a Viking settlement was uncovered in L'Anse Aux Meadows in northern Newfoundland proving the Vikings had indeed reached America. However, this area was no land of wine – so where is Vinland? Nobody can be sure of its exact location, though experts believe it must lie somewhere along the coastline of what is now eastern or northeastern Canada.

A reconstruction of a Viking house at L'Anse Aux Meadows.

MERCHANTS AND TRADERS

THE VIKINGS were skilled merchants, buying and selling goods – and slaves – far beyond their shores. At home, they founded the great trading cities of Hedeby in Denmark, Birka in Sweden and Kaupang in Norway. As they settled new lands, Viking trade routes spread far and wide. Merchants sold goods such as timber, iron, animal furs and ivory walrus tusks. In exchange they bought luxuries such as woollen cloth from the British Isles, wines from France and Germany, and gold and pottery from the Mediterranean.

Merchants carried balance scales like these to weigh coins.

Viking merchants prepare for a long journey as their ships are loaded with goods to trade.

It was my grandfather who first discovered these ancient Viking coins. I did not lay eyes upon them again till after his death, and when I did I could well understand his excitement in holding them. What incredible journeys did these tokens make, and through what hands did they pass?

Robert Macleod

The Vikings traded as far east as Baghdad.

KEY TO TRADED GOODS

- Timber
- Walrus Tusks
- Slaves
- Honey
- Wool
- Furs
- Pottery
- Silk
- Wine
- Silver
- Spices

NORWAY

SWEDEN

Baltic Sea

BRITISH ISLES

Kaupang

Birka

Novgorod

DENMARK

Dublin

York

RUSSIA

Hedeby

Kiev

GERMANY

Paris

FRANCE

Black Sea

Constantinople

Baghdad

Mediterranean Sea

Travelling East

As Viking trade spread east across the Baltic Sea and down the rivers of Eastern Europe, trading centres were set up in places like Novgorod and Kiev. As these towns flourished, they became powerful states ruled by Swedish chieftains. The Slavic people called the Vikings "Rus" - from which the name "Russia" comes. Eventually the Vikings made the journey across the Black Sea to Constantinople (Istanbul) and further east to Baghdad. From these far-flung cities, the Vikings brought back silver coins, exotic spices and silk fabrics.

Ninth-century silk from Constantinople.

Spices such as cinnamon were brought back from distant lands.

VIKING ATTACK!

Many a time I have gazed across the sea and imagined the coming of the Vikings. What would it have been like to come face to face with those battle-scarred warriors? I imagine people cowered as strange shouts and curses reached their ears, while others watched helplessly as the invaders waded ashore. Armed with swords and axes, Vikings would have torn through the village looting and killing at will. And then the raiders would have been gone, the memory of their violence a very curse upon the land...

Tom Macleod

(An extract from the diary of Tom Macleod)

VIKING WARRIORS

THE SAGAS tell of the Vikings' great courage and daring in battle – the greatest honour of all for a warrior was to die by the sword. They were fearless fighters and it was the Vikings' legendary bravery that often helped them to victory. Boys were trained in the use of weapons from an early age and as adults could be called up to fight at any time. Early Vikings were loyal to a local lord but in later times, warriors fought for their king and were organized into armies.

A Swedish rune stone showing Viking warriors aboard a warship.

"...I know one thing that never dies, the glory of the great dead."

– from the Viking poem, "Hávamál"

Terrifying Beserkers

Most feared of all Viking warriors were the "beserkers". As one Icelandic saga describes them, beserkers were as "mad as dogs or wolves... and were as strong as bears or wild oxen". Working themselves into a frenzied rage before battle, these fearsome warriors terrified their victims by howling like beasts, biting their shields and frothing at the mouth.

A richly decorated axehead discovered in a Viking grave in Mammen, Denmark.

Towards the end of the Viking age, warriors began to fight on horseback. This mounted warrior is from the Baldishol Tapestry in Norway.

The Glorious Dead

In Norse legends, female warriors called Valkyries flew over the battlefields gathering up the souls of the dead before carrying them to Valhalla, a majestic banquet hall ruled over by the god Odin. Here, slain warriors feasted and prepared for "Ragnarök", the great battle that the Vikings believed would take place between the gods and the forces of evil.

A Valkyrie flies across the battlefield.

RAIDING THE WEST

IN 793 AD, Viking warriors ran their longboats ashore on Lindisfarne (an island off the east coast of England) and attacked the Christian monastery there. Terrified, the monks desperately tried to fend off the Vikings, but they were brutally slaughtered and the buildings left in ruins as the warriors escaped with the monastery's treasures. This was the start of the Vikings' long reign of terror across Europe.

Viking Conquerors

At first, the Vikings fought in small groups raiding easy coastal targets during the summer months. However, they soon became more daring, spending the winters in places they had captured. The Vikings sailed up the rivers of Europe and attacked great cities such as Paris and Hamburg. Across the British Isles, they established themselves as rulers in areas they had attacked, and in the north west of France the area around Rouen became known as Normandy ("Land of the Northmen"). Viking fleets even sailed as far as the Mediterranean, raiding the coasts of Spain, Italy and North Africa.

This stone from Lindisfarne is thought to show Viking raiders attacking the island's monastery in 793 AD.

The priory that stands at Lindisfarne today was built on top of the ruins left by the Vikings.

The Terror of Europe

Viking raids were swift and ruthless, and usually came as a total surprise. Warriors would appear suddenly on their longboats and storm ashore. Well armed and fearsomely brave, the Vikings nearly always got what they wanted, and the lightning speed of their attacks made fighting back almost impossible for the unfortunate victims. However, during the second half of the ninth century, European leaders began to build defences such as castles and fortresses to resist invasion.

The speed and brutality of the Vikings' attacks made it difficult for their victims to fight back.

The Danegeld

European leaders were desperate to stop the Vikings' violence. In 845 AD, the French king, Charles the Bald, paid an enormous sum of silver to the Viking leader Ragnar Hairy-Breeks to make him leave Paris. During the tenth century, English kings began to pay huge sums to Danish Vikings known as Danegeld. These bribes didn't work though - the Vikings took the money, but repeatedly returned for more riches.

Millions of Anglo-Saxon coins were handed over to the Vikings as Danegeld bribes.

An eighth-century Anglo-Saxon helmet from York, a city which was conquered by the Vikings.

ERIC BLOODAXE

ERIC BLOODAXE was the ruler of the Viking kingdom of Northumbria in England. The son of the Norwegian king Harald Finehair, Eric is said to have started his fighting life aged 12. According to the sagas, he was a ruthless warrior, his savagery shocking even his fellow Vikings. However, other sources suggest Eric was under the thumb of his evil wife, Gunnhild, and blame his harsh rule on her wicked influence.

 38

A Bloodthirsty Murderer

The eldest and favourite son of his father, Eric earned his fearsome nickname by slaying his four brothers in order to take the Norwegian throne for himself. However, he was a ruthless and unpopular king, and his surviving brother, Hakon the Good, sailed from England to Norway to claim the throne. Eric fled to England where he became king of Northumbria with a palace in the capital city of York.

King of Northumbria

In 947 AD, Eadred, King of England, launched an attack on Northumbria to fight off his Viking rival. As Eadred's soldiers moved south again, Eric Bloodaxe's soldiers caught up with them and slaughtered many. In revenge, Eadred promised to destroy Northumbria and succeeded in persuading its people to reject Eric's rule. However, when the Dublin Viking Olaf Sihtricson took control of Northumbria in 952 AD, Eric Bloodaxe responded furiously by seizing the throne for a second time. His rule did not last long though, and in 954 AD he was killed at the battle of Stainmore. His death marked the end of Viking rule at York.

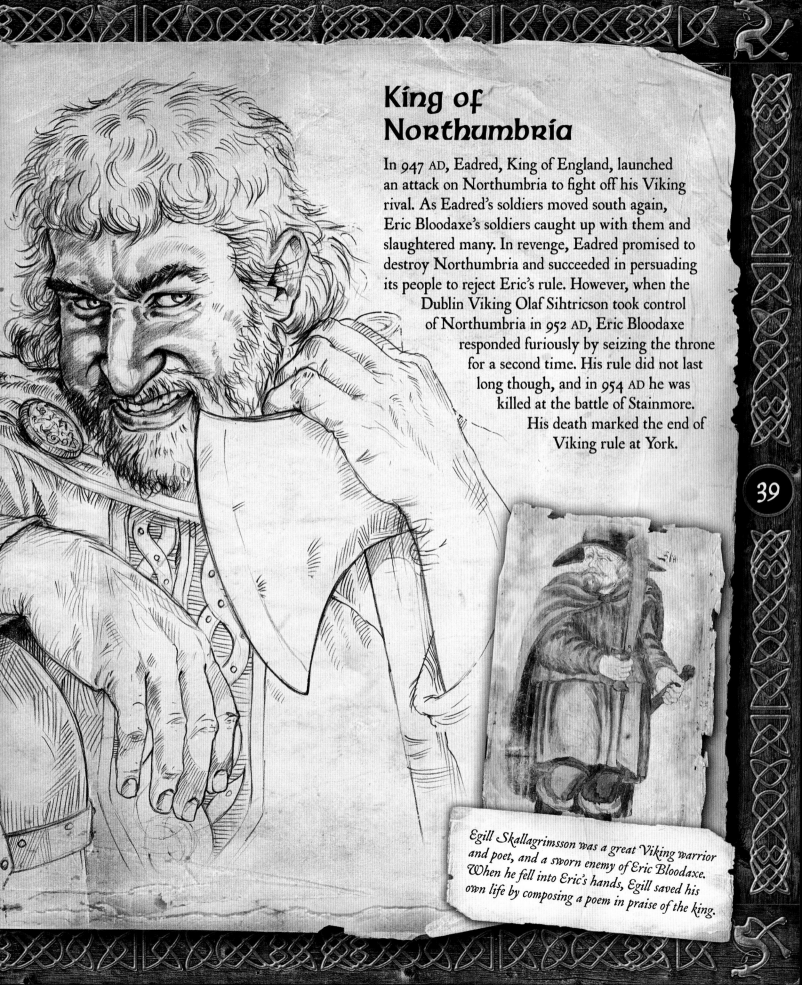

Egill Skallagrimsson was a great Viking warrior and poet, and a sworn enemy of Eric Bloodaxe. When he fell into Eric's hands, Egill saved his own life by composing a poem in praise of the king.

Armour

Unlike modern soldiers, Viking warriors did not wear a uniform but dressed and armed themselves. Many wore leather tunics and hard leather caps for battle, although these would not have prevented injury from sharpened swords and arrows. Chain-mail shirts made from interlocking iron rings and metal helmets gave much better protection, but were expensive and probably only worn by rich and powerful leaders.

Helmets and Shields

Very few helmets have survived from the Viking age. Made from iron,
they had rounded or pointed tops, and an eye and nose guard or just a simple
nose-bar. Warriors carried round wooden shields that protected most of the
body. Up to 1 metre across, they would have been painted and may have been
covered in leather. An iron knob in the centre known as the "boss" protected
the warrior's hand. Since wood rots, the boss is usually the only part of the
shield that archaeologists ever find.

WEAPONRY

A WARRIOR'S most treasured possession was undoubtedly his sword, though he needed to be trained to fight with a variety of weapons. Dead Vikings were often buried with their weapons – a beautiful sword, richly decorated with silver and gold, showed that its owner was wealthy and powerful.

Bows and Arrows

Wooden bows and iron-tipped arrows were used for hunting and sometimes in battle. Bolt-like arrowheads could pierce through chain mail causing lethal injuries.

Spears

Warriors carried different sizes of spear. Lightweight throwing spears or javelins could be thrown at the enemy, while heavier thrusting spears with broader blades were used in close combat.

Battle Axes

The Vikings used a variety of axes in battle. Some could be thrown from a distance, and others were used to hack at an enemy in close hand-to-hand fighting. Axes were long-handled with broad blades. When used with two hands, the axe was a weapon of terror for it could cut through armour, and slice off heads and limbs.

Knives

Most warriors carried a small, single-edged knife with a handle made from bone or wood. This was usually carried in a leather sheaf attached to a belt. The knife was an essential everyday tool but could also be used in close fighting.

SWORDS

WARRIORS treasured their swords and often gave them names such as "Leg-biter" or "Fierce". A Viking sword had a double-edged blade that was strong as well as flexible, meaning it would not shatter when struck by the enemy. The sword's hilt (handle) was often beautifully decorated.

When this once-magnificent sword first emerged from its ancient resting place, I shivered to think upon the battles it had seen. Whose hands once gripped the decorated hilt, and was this weapon perhaps named to celebrate the strength and sharpness of its blade?

Robert Macleod

LIFE IN VIKING TIMES

Well over a thousand years have past since Vikings first settled these parts. Here they found fresh water as well as rich farmland and plentiful stone for building their houses. They were warriors before all, but the settlers were also farmers, skilled craftsmen and storytellers. I imagine a family gathered around the warm hearth of their longhouse sharing the tales and legends of their homeland. The Vikings tried to make this land their own — and indeed, echoes of their language and customs linger still...

Tom Macleod

(An extract from the diary of Tom Macleod)

JARLS AND KARLS

VIKING SOCIETY was divided into three main classes. At the top of the social pyramid was the king along with noble landowners called "jarls". Beneath the jarls were the "karls" or "freemen" who were usually farmers, merchants, craftsmen or warriors. The lowest of the low were the slaves known as "thralls". Slaves had no rights at all – they could be bought and sold like property, and were often captured in raids and battles.

Jarl

Karl

Thrall

In Viking society, power was held by the jarls. Most people were karls who owned or rented some land. The thralls at the bottom of the heap had no freedoms at all.

Kings and Kingdoms

In early Viking times, Scandinavia was divided into small kingdoms ruled over by local kings and jarls. Rulers were expected to protect their communities but often struggled to keep power. The Vikings held open-air meetings called "Things" where important issues were discussed – any free person could take part. However, over time kings became more and more powerful and the importance of these meetings began to lessen. By 880 AD, Harald Finehair had brought all of Norway under his reign, and by the end of the tenth century, powerful kings ruled over Denmark and Sweden too.

Vikings take part in a discussion at the Thing.

Family Feuds

A Viking's honour and good name were highly valued, and family ties were very important. Men were prepared to fight to the death if it meant protecting their family's reputation, and disputes were often settled by duels. Violent blood-feuds between families often lasted for generations.

Crime and Punishment

People suspected of crimes were sometimes forced to take tests called "ordeals". Stones had to be picked out of boiling water or red-hot iron carried for several seconds. The Vikings believed that the gods would help the innocent and so those who failed the tests were considered guilty. The Thing usually decided a criminal's punishment – he or she might be fined, banished from society or forced to become a slave.

This engraved arm ring belonged to a high-ranking Viking.

FARMS AND TOWNS

IN VIKING TIMES, most people were farmers and hunters who lived in the countryside. Animals such as sheep, pigs and cows were raised for food and milk, and crops such as barley and wheat were grown. Conditions in the Viking homelands could be very difficult – the weather was often bitterly cold and in Norway there was a lack of good farmland. This is one of the reasons why the Vikings left their shores in search of new lands.

This reconstructed Viking village is at Hedeby, Germany. Once part of Denmark, Hedeby was a great Viking town.

Sheep and cattle were farmed for their milk and meat.

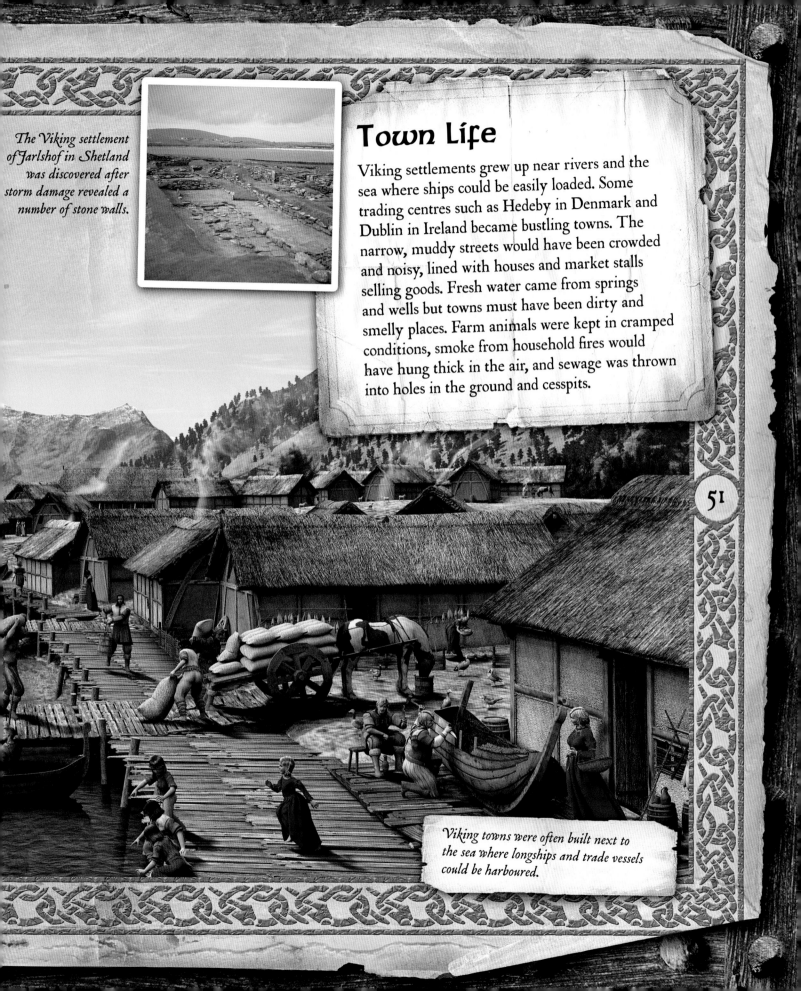

The Viking settlement of Jarlshof in Shetland was discovered after storm damage revealed a number of stone walls.

Town Life

Viking settlements grew up near rivers and the sea where ships could be easily loaded. Some trading centres such as Hedeby in Denmark and Dublin in Ireland became bustling towns. The narrow, muddy streets would have been crowded and noisy, lined with houses and market stalls selling goods. Fresh water came from springs and wells but towns must have been dirty and smelly places. Farm animals were kept in cramped conditions, smoke from household fires would have hung thick in the air, and sewage was thrown into holes in the ground and cesspits.

Viking towns were often built next to the sea where longships and trade vessels could be harboured.

THE VIKINGS AT HOME

MOST VIKING FAMILIES lived in long, low farmhouses consisting of one main room. Depending on the region and materials available, houses were built of stone, wood or turf, and often had thatched or turf roofs. Floors consisted of flattened earth, and walls could be made of "wattle" (branches woven together), which was smeared with mud or dung to keep out the wind and rain.

Viking women looked after the household keys.

Home Comforts

Most Viking homes would have been very crowded with three or more generations living under one roof. Houses were dark and smoky with only a dim light given out by the cooking fire and lamps hung on ropes. In the bitterly cold winters, many families were forced to share their living space with farm animals that were penned in at one end of the house.

A reconstruction of a Viking home at L'Anse aux Meadows, Canada. Interior posts support a heavy sod roof made of earth.

A reconstructed Viking home in Iceland. Houses here were usually built from stone and turf.

Food was prepared in clay cooking pots like this one.

Around the Hearth

Although building materials varied, the layout of houses was similar across the Viking world. At the centre of the home was a large fireplace with a hole in the ceiling above through which smoke could escape. Raised platforms along the walls were used for sitting and sleeping. Wealthier homes usually had smaller rooms on each side of the main hall that could be used as bedrooms, store rooms or kitchens, and the richest Vikings might own wooden chairs and beds. Weapons and tools were hung from the roof, valued belongings hidden away in locked chests, and foodstuffs were stored in barrels.

FAMILY LIFE

In Viking times, family ties were strong. A man was head of his household, but women took charge when their husbands were away. Children didn't go to school, but instead helped in the fields and with cooking, weaving and spinning. Families and communities needed to provide for themselves, and children learnt important skills from a young age.

Over a thousand years have passed since this buckle fastened a warrior's belt. Made of bronze and dulled by the passing centuries, it was likely once decorated to show its owner's importance.

Robert Macleod

All Vikings wore leather footwear.

Viking Fashions

The style of clothing changed very little during the Viking age. Men wore woollen trousers and linen shirts, and over these a long-sleeved tunic and belt. When the weather was cold, heavy cloaks and furs kept them warm. Viking women clothed themselves in long dresses, and apron-like overdresses fastened with a pair of brooches. Outside they might cover up with shawls and long woollen cloaks. Both men and women wore flat leather shoes or boots. The wealthy could afford richly coloured cloths and beautiful gold and silver jewellery. Poorer Vikings made do with plain garments and ornaments made from bronze or copper.

Viking women were skilled spinners and weavers. They used vertical looms similar to this one to weave plain or patterned cloth.

A tenth-century gold brooch from Denmark.

Barley

Meal Time

The Vikings had two main meals a day, one in the morning and one in the evening. Those who lived near the sea ate fish such as herring and cod daily. Fish and meat such as beef or pork were salted, smoked over fires or dried outside to preserve them. Wild animals such as boar and deer were hunted, as were seals, walruses and whales. The Vikings ate a lot of porridge made from barley and oats, and barley bread. Beer was made from barley and hops, and people also enjoyed an alcoholic drink made from honey called "mead".

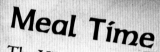

Fish and meat were salted and dried in the sun to preserve them.

FEASTING AND FUN

FEASTS were an important part of Viking life, and a chance to forget the darkness and bitter cold of the winter months. Weddings and religious festivals were celebrated, along with the arrival of summer and the coming of harvest time. People dressed in their finest clothes, and tables were laden with food and drink. At feasts held by wealthy Vikings, music was played and poets called Skalds entertained the guests with thrilling tales and legends.

56

Food was stewed in large cauldrons hung over the fire.

Games and Leisure

During the warmth of summer, people swam and went boating, while sledging and skiing were enjoyed in the winter. Wrestling and archery were popular sports, and many enjoyed betting on horse fights. During the long, dark evenings, people gathered around the fire to tell stories and sing songs. The Vikings delighted in board games – "hneftafl" was a favourite, and involved one player using his eight pieces to protect the king from the 16 pieces of another player.

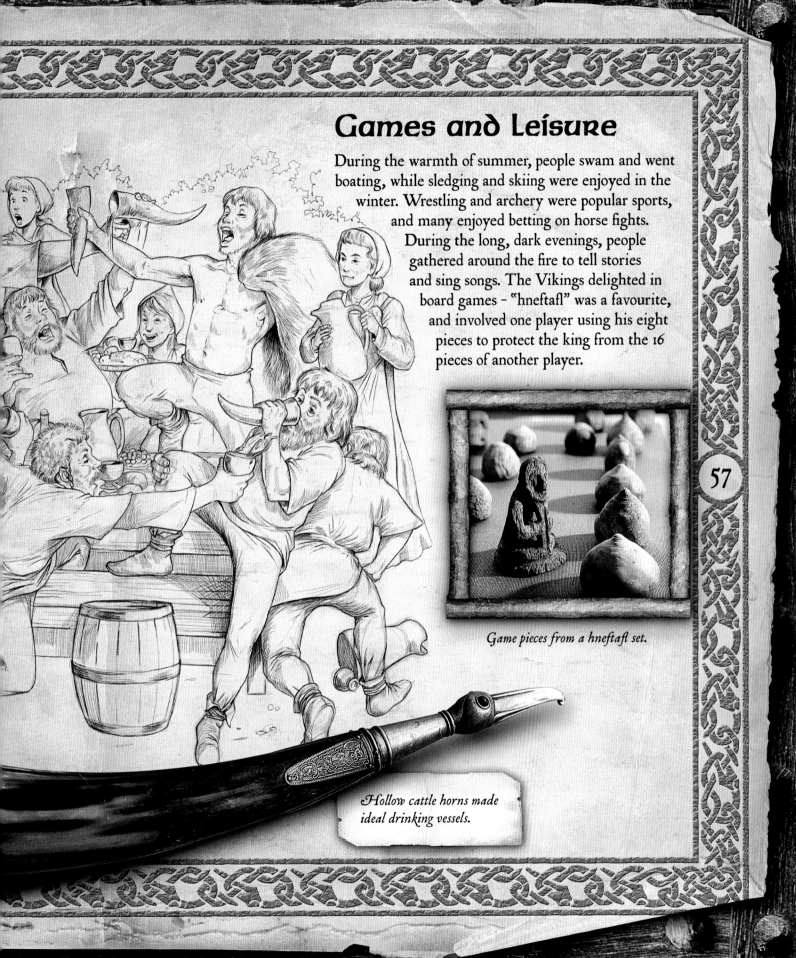

Game pieces from a hneftafl set.

Hollow cattle horns made ideal drinking vessels.

Viking Crafts

The Vikings were skilled craftsmen, expert at shipbuilding, metalworking and woodwork. In every home, essential tools were made and repaired while women spun and wove to make the family's clothes. Both men and women wore jewellery and many beautifully crafted pieces have been discovered. Gold and silver were a sign of wealth, while cheaper pieces were made from bronze, copper, carved animal bones and coloured glass.

Viking Gold

Both men and women wore rings like this gold piece (right). This mount to put a horse's bridle on (left), is made of bronze covered in gold leaf.

Animal Bone

Skilled craftsmen carved intricate patterns into animal bone. This carving from Denmark is thought to be the bone handle of a walking stick.

Necklace

This beautiful rock crystal pendant was discovered in Gotland, Sweden. Wearing expensive jewellery was a sign of wealth and status.

Carved Wood

A detail showing the beautiful wood carvings on the stern of the Oseberg ship. This ship burial was one of the finest Viking finds ever made.

Metalwork

This stunning brooch is from Aker, Norway. It's made from silver-plated iron inlaid with precious stones.

LEGEND AND LORE

Last night, a shrieking gale rolled in from the sea. For some reason I took out the box containing the nails and coins I found — it seems strange to say, but I fancied the objects quivered in my hand. Later, terrible dreams disturbed my sleep. I was aware of a god-like warrior figure, his voice like thunder, and a truly monstrous serpent that reared up from a dark sea. I awoke exhausted and with the certain knowledge that the spirits of long-dead Vikings haunt this land. More than ever, I am determined to find the grave that surely lies nearby...

Tom Macleod

(An extract from the diary of Tom Macleod)

THE VIKING UNIVERSE

THE VIKINGS believed the universe was ruled over by many gods and goddesses, and that amazing creatures lived in its various parts. At the centre of the universe was Yggdrasil, an ash tree that held everything together. Humans lived in Midgard, which was surrounded by an ocean containing a giant serpent. The gods were found in Asgard and Vanaheim, while giants, trolls and other dreadful beings lived in separate kingdoms. At the bottom of the tree was Niflheim, an icy place of eternal darkness.

The Chief Gods

The most important Viking god was Odin, whose one eye was said to blaze like the sun. The god of war and wisdom, Odin was thought to possess many amazing powers. Thor, the god of thunder, was incredibly strong though not as clever as Odin. Happy to take on any challenge, Thor once held a drinking contest with giants and swallowed so much sea that the tide went out. Frey was the god of fertility and birth. People called on him for good crops, and hoped for his blessing when they got married.

Frey was believed to bring good fortune.

Vanaheim, the world of the "Vanir" gods

Bifrost, the burning rainbow bridge connecting Midgard and Asgard

Svartalfheim, the land of the dark elves

Nidavellir, the land of the dwarfs

Muspell, the world of fire

Asgard, the world of the most
important "Aesir" gods

Rituals and Sacrifice

Religious ceremonies were usually held in the
open air. Gifts such as weapons and jewellery
were offered to the gods – these have been found
preserved in bogs where they were thrown.
Animals and even people were also sacrificed to
the gods. Some graves have been found to contain
the bodies of people who were probably killed to
accompany the person being buried.

Valhalla, the majestic hall
ruled over by the god Odin

The Shapeshifting God

The mischievous Loki was part god and part
devil. In one legend, Loki foolishly entered a bet
with two dwarfs to see who could create the most
wonderful treasures for the gods. Loki transformed
himself into a fly and tried to distract his rivals,
stinging them as they worked. However, the
dwarfs still won the bet and Loki was punished
by having his mouth sewn shut.

Alfheim, the land of
the light elves

Midgard, or Earth, the
realm of human beings

Jotunheim, the land of
the giants

Niflheim, the icy underworld
of the dead

This tenth-century forge stone discovered on a Danish beach
shows Loki with his lips sewn together.

RUNES

THE VIKINGS developed a way of writing using marks or letters called runes. The 16 letters were made up of straight and diagonal lines so that brief messages could easily be carved into stone, bone and wood. The Viking alphabet was known as "futhark" after the first six sounds. Glorious battles and heroic warriors were celebrated in memorial stones known as rune stones, which have been found across the Viking world. The word "runes" means something secret or hidden, and Vikings thought runes had their own powerful magic.

f	u	th	a
r	k	h	n
i	a	s	t
b	m	l	R

A picture stone from Gotland, Sweden. Odin's eight-legged horse, Sleipnir, can be seen carrying the god.

This is the Danish version of the "futhark". Runes were often used in magic - for example, the arrow shaped letter "tyr", named after the god Tyr, was sometimes carved on weapons in the hope that this god would bring victory in battle.

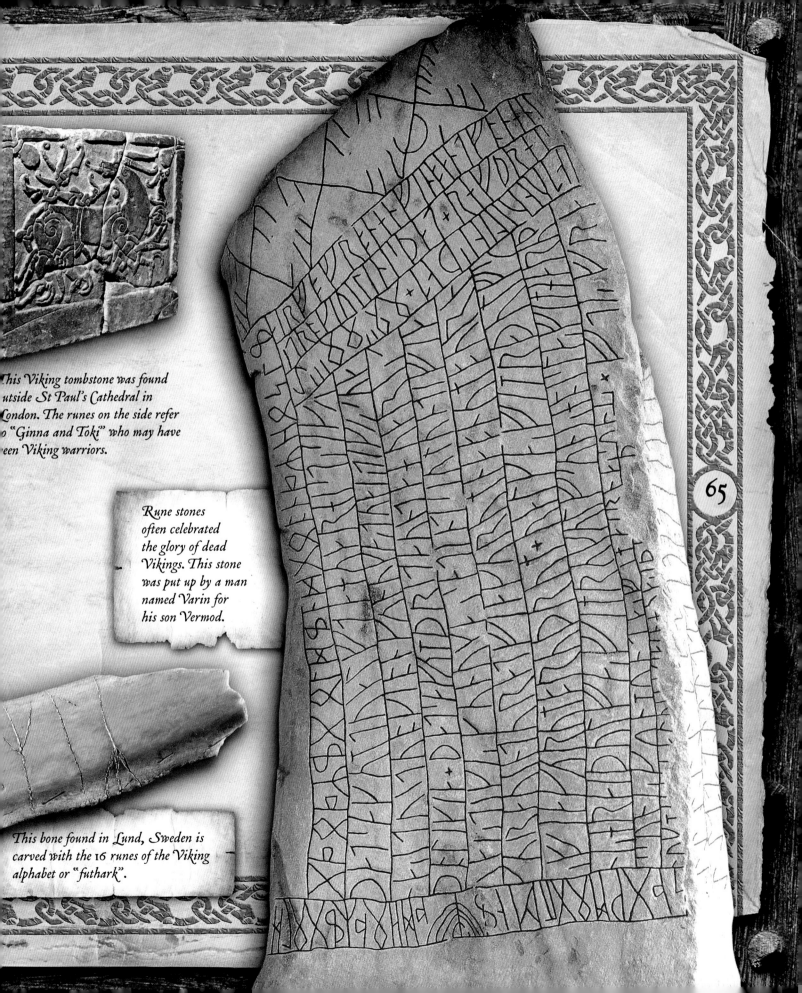

This Viking tombstone was found outside St Paul's Cathedral in London. The runes on the side refer to "Ginna and Toki" who may have been Viking warriors.

Rune stones often celebrated the glory of dead Vikings. This stone was put up by a man named Varin for his son Vermod.

This bone found in Lund, Sweden is carved with the 16 runes of the Viking alphabet or "futhark".

THE
JELLING STONE

THIS DETAIL (below) is a copy from one of two rune stones discovered at Jelling in Jutland, Denmark. The three-sided stone was raised by the Danish king Harald Bluetooth in honour of his royal parents over 1,200 years ago. An inscription on one side reads: "King Harald commanded this monument to be made in memory of Gorm his father and in memory of Thyre his mother – that Harald who won the whole of Denmark for himself and made the Danes Christian". The figure shown here is the earliest Scandinavian image of Jesus Christ – Harald became a Christian around 960 AD.

SAGAS AND LEGENDS

THE VIKINGS loved to tell each other thrilling legends of gods and monsters, and tales of heroic warriors and battles. Some stories recounted the adventures of kings while others were gripping accounts of ordinary families. The legends weren't written down by the Vikings themselves – it was not until the thirteenth century that writers began to record these stories in books called sagas.

The Story of Burnt Njal

This famous saga about an Icelandic family has much to tell us about Viking beliefs. Honour was all-important and minor disagreements could result in years of bloodshed. The tale is about two friends Gunnar and Njal. Their close friendship is tested when Gunnar, a powerful warrior, marries an evil widow who begins a deadly feud with Njal's wife. As the conflict spreads far beyond the family, the wise and peace-loving Njal frequently attempts to make amends but eventually Gunnar is murdered. The second half of the saga centres upon Njal and his sons. As they seek revenge for Gunnar's death, the men are led down a dark and dangerous path until finally spiteful Icelanders set their home on fire and they are killed in the flames.

An illustration depicting the saga of Burnt Njal. Vengeful Icelanders look on as Njal's house is set on fire.

This beautifully carved pendant was surely once treasured. In Norse myths, Thor's hammer defended both gods and humans from harm. I imagine this silver relic hanging around its owner's neck - on stormy seas and in battle, did he feel certain of Thor's protection?

Robert Macleod

68

The Theft of Thor's Hammer

One morning the mighty god Thor awakes to discover that his powerful hammer, Mjollnir, has been stolen. The thief is Thrym, king of the giants, who says he will only return the hammer if the beautiful goddess Freya marries him. The gods hatch a plan and agree that Thor should dress as Freya with Loki disguised as her bridesmaid. The two set out for Thrym's castle where they are welcomed with a feast. Thor almost gives himself away by consuming an entire ox but Loki assures Thrym that Freya is just hungry. When the giant lifts his bride's veil to kiss her, he is alarmed at her burning eyes. However, Loki tells Thrym that Freya is merely tired - excited about her wedding, she has not slept or eaten for eight days. As the giant fetches the magic hammer to bless the marriage, Thor seizes his prized weapon and sets about beating Thrym and several other giants to death.

Thor beating the giants to death.

THE MIDGARD SERPENT

IN VIKING MYTHS, the god Loki had three monstrous children: the wolf Fenrir, the dreadful goddess Hel, and Jormungand, a giant serpent also known as the Midgard Serpent. Even the gods were afraid of Jormungand, and Odin decided to get rid of this terrible creature by tossing it into the ocean. Here the serpent grew so large that eventually it encircled the entire world. Sailors venturing across the seas were ever fearful that the Midgard Serpent would rise up from the ocean depths and crush their ships in its massive jaws or destroy them with its deadly venom.

A VIKING BURIAL

THE VIKINGS believed in the afterlife and so they buried their dead with all kinds of objects that might be needed in the next world. Prized weapons, tools, clothes and jewellery were all common grave goods. Ordinary people were buried in simple graves, often beneath an earth mound, but wealthier Vikings were frequently buried in boats or ships to carry them safely to the afterlife. Sometimes the vessel was set alight and burnt in a funeral pyre. Animals and even slaves were sacrificed and buried with important Vikings.

The impressive figurehead of the Oseberg burial ship found in Norway.

Lindholm Høje is a dramatic burial site overlooking the Danish city of Aalborg. It contains nearly 700 graves from the Iron and Viking Ages.

A Ship Fit for a Queen

In 1903, archaeologists uncovered a beautiful ship at the Oseberg burial mound near Oslo in Norway. Like the Gokstad ship discovered in 1880, blue clay surrounding the vessel had preserved it. The ship was made almost entirely of oak, and the prow and stern were finely decorated with carvings of animals.

At the centre of the boat was a wooden grave chamber containing the remains of two women believed to be a queen and her maid. The ship contained many fine objects including a full set of 30 oars, beds, four sleighs, a beautifully decorated wagon and a loom.

Beautiful carvings cover the prow and stern of the Oseberg ship.

This bearded head was carved on a post on the wagon found inside the Oseberg ship.

The richly decorated wagon discovered within the Oseberg ship.

HARALD HARDRADA

ONE OF THE MOST feared rulers in Europe, Harald Hardrada was the king of Norway from 1046 to 1066. His true name was Harald Sigurdsson, but the king's reputation for crushing enemies earned him the nickname Hardrada or "the Ruthless". Harald ruled his kingdom with an iron first but first and foremost he was a warrior, a man who showed no mercy to those he conquered.

Harald the Ruthless

Harald was the half-brother of the Norwegian king Olaf Haraldsson. In 1030, when he was just 15, he fought with his brother at the battle of Stiklestad where Olaf was defeated. Harald escaped from Norway to the Russian state of Kiev and became a military commander. Later, he fought for the Byzantine Empire and made a fortune through raiding. In 1045, Harald returned to his homeland and became joint ruler with his nephew, King Magnus. When Magnus died in 1047, Harald became all-powerful and now made a claim for Denmark's throne. He spent the next 20 years raiding that country's coast and repeatedly fighting its king.

The Last Viking

In 1066, Harald Hardrada set off on his last great campaign to conquer England. Leading a fleet of 300 ships across the North Sea, he won a brutal battle at Fulford. From here the Viking king marched his army towards Stamford Bridge, but he was surprised there by the English king who had rapidly moved his army north. In the battle that followed, Harald was killed. Although occasional Viking attacks on England took place after this time, many historians view 1066 as the end of the Viking age, and Harald is often seen as the last great Viking.

The Battle of Stamford Bridge pitted the forces of the English king Harold Godwinson against those of Harald Hardrada.

Battle Relics

Just outside the Viking city of York, close to the road that led to Fulford, a church cemetery was discovered containing 11 skeletons of young men. Upon their bones were the terrible scars of battle injuries. Might these be the remains of the Anglo-Saxon soldiers who died defending their land from Harald Hardrada's Viking army? If so, a mystery surrounds their burial: more than 1,500 probably died on the battlefield, so why have so few graves been discovered?

THE LAST VIKINGS

DURING THE ELEVENTH CENTURY, Viking raids became less successful as European leaders built up armies and defended their territories. In Scandinavia, the spread of Christianity led to more stability and people began to reject old ideas. Raiding was no longer encouraged by powerful Scandinavian kings and elsewhere Viking settlers became part of new communities with different beliefs and traditions.

The Coming of the Normans

In 1066, the defeat of Harald Hardrada at the Battle of Stamford Bridge came to symbolize the death of Viking power. In the same year, the Normans - who were in fact descendants of Viking settlers in Normandy - invaded England, and William "the Conqueror" took the English throne. Norse raids did not altogether stop at this point, though they became much less common. The great age of Vikings was drawing to a close, though the Viking spirit lives on in sagas and legends.

A scene from the Bayeux Tapestry showing the Norman invasion of England.

This Christian cross has a dragon's head - the old Viking beliefs were slow to die out.

The Norwegian king Olaf II Haraldsson attempted to convert his people to Christianity. Known as Olaf the Stout during his lifetime, after his death he was made the patron saint of Norway.

The Gosforth Cross mixes scenes from the Bible with Viking mythology.

As Christianity took hold in Scandinavia, wooden churches began to appear built from upright planks (staves). This is the Borgund Stave Church in Norway dating from around 1180.

Acknowledgements

It was my grandfather's stirring tales of lightning-swift dragon boats and battle-scarred warriors that first stirred my interest in the Vikings. However, it was not until the incredible discovery of Tom Macleod's journal and the Viking grave that lay so close to his home that I set out on the fascinating path of research that would eventually lead to the writing of this book.

As well as saluting the passion and dedication of my grandfather, I would like to pay tribute to the following people who have made this project possible: my editor Selina Wood for her encouragement and helpful insights; the consultant Peter Chrisp for his careful reading and expert advice; Jake da'Costa and Russell Porter for their imaginative art direction; Luke Wijesveld for his exceptional design; Kira Hagen and Anthony Arndt for their invaluable supply of re-enactment images and helpful advice; Larry Rostant for his unique and stunning illustration; Mark Millmore for the wonderful CGI illustration work; Mark Walker for Photoshop wizardry; Leo Brown for his superb character drawings; Paul Langan for his thorough picture research; Ena Matagic for her exacting production; and finally the archaeologist Heidi Scott who excavated the Viking grave site with meticulous care and provided such fascinating insights into the objects unearthed.

ROBERT MACLEOD lives on the remote Scottish coastline and has a passionate interest in the Viking age. His inspiration comes from an old journal belonging to his grandfather Tom Macleod, which documents the discovery of long forgotten Viking relics.

80

PICTURE CREDITS

The publishers would like to thank the following sources for their kind permission to reproduce the pictures in this book.
Key, T =top, L=left, R=right, C=centre, B=bottom.

akg-images: /Bildarchiv Monheim: 55TR; /Interfoto: 6BR, 44L, 77TL; /Erich Lessing: 21R; /Sambraus: 22BL
The Art Archive: /Collection Dagli Orti: 65R; /Gianni Dagli Orti: 66-67; /Historiska Museet Stockholm/Collection Dagli Orti: 13TR, 30TR; /Prehistoric Museum Moessgard Hojbjerg, Denmark/Gianni Dagli Orti: 17BL (shears and comb)
Flemming Bau: 26C
Bridgeman Art Library: /Ancient Art and Architecture Collection Ltd.: 12TR, 34L, 54-55B, 64BL; /Arni Magnusson Institute, Reykjavik, Iceland: 39BR; /Neil Holmes: 34BL; /Kunstindustrimuseet, Oslo, Norway: 31BR; /National Museums of Scotland: 31TC; /Nationalmuseet, Copenhagen, Denmark: 31L; /Private Collection: 35TL; /O. Vaering: 75R; /Viking Ship Museum, Oslo, Norway: 72L; /Werner Forman Archive: 17BL (coins), 59C
Carlton Books: 40T, 41; /Kira Hagen: 1BKG, 13TC, 30B, 32-33, 38, 43L, 43C, 44R-45, 56-57B, 74BR; /Larry Rostant: 1C, 2-3, 8, 12L, 28, 36-37
Corbis: /Dave Bartruff/Genesis Photos: 53TR; /Walter Bibikow: 76BL; /Christophe Boisvieux: 20-21C; /Ashley Cooper: 50BL; /Roland Gerth: 13C, 22BC, 55BR; /Heritage Images: 20L; /Chris Hills/Demotix: 56BL; /Yves Marcoux/First Light: 25BR; /Ted Spiegel: 6BC, 26BL, 50L, 52L, 72B; /Tim Thompson: 52BL; /Werner Forman: 35BL, 53B, 59L, 59R
Getty Images: /Bridgeman Art Library: 58R, 77TR; /Sissie Brimberg/National Geographic: 20TR; /Andy Crawford/Dorling Kindersley: 12C, 29, 40B; /Rachid Dahnoun: 60; /De Agostini Picture Library/Dagli Orti: 27BR, 62BL; /Danita Delimont/Gallo Images: 35BR, 50C; /John Elk/Lonely Planet Images: 67R; /Hulton Archive: 17TL; /David Lomax/Robert Harding: 51TC; /Gary Ombler/Dorling Kindersley: 42L (bow and arrows); /Universal Image Group/Werner Forman: 6BL, 12BR, 16BR, 17R, 17BL (arm ring), 23TR, 26TR, 42BR, 55C, 57R, 58L, 58BR, 63BR, 68BL, 73L, 77BR; /Duncan Walker: 31R
Media Militia: 7TR
Scala Picture Library: /De Agostini Picture Library: 48-49B, 64-65B; /Metropolitan Museum: 7BL, 54BL
Thinkstock: 23BR, 24B, 27BC, 55BC, 78-79
Topfoto: 76R; /The Grainger Collection: 65TL; /ImageWorks: 73R; /Stapleton Historical Collection/Heritage-Images: 68R
University of Oslo: /Museum of Cultural History: 73BR
Viking Ship Museum, Roskilde, Denmark: 20-21B
Wiki Commons: /16L

Every effort has been made to acknowledge correctly and contact the source and/or copyright holder of each picture and Carlton Books Limited apologises for any unintentional errors or omissions, which will be corrected in future editions of this book.